D1124131

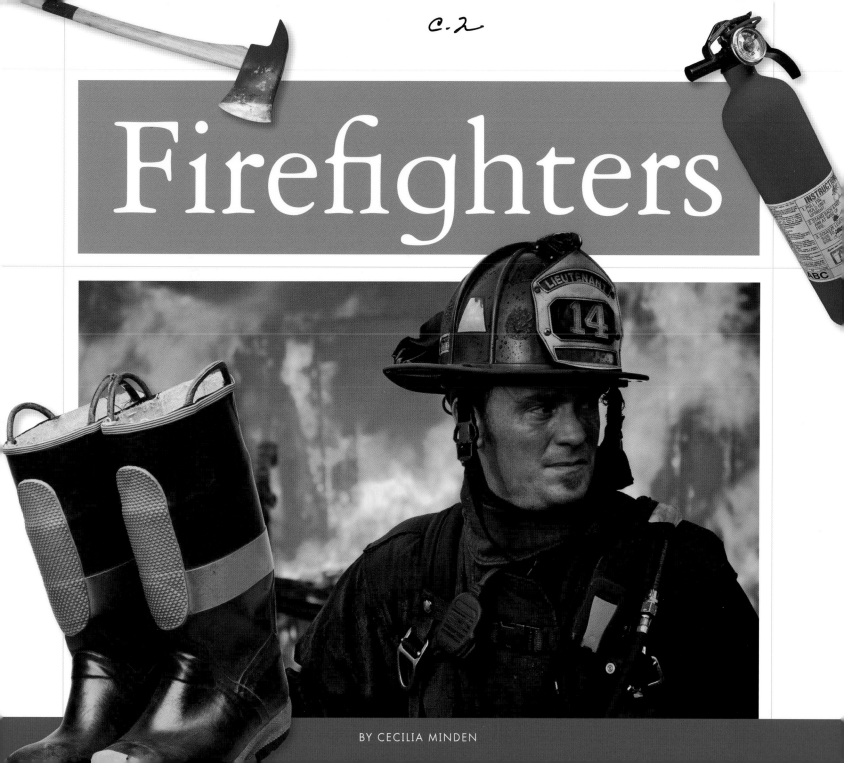

Firefighters

BY CECILIA MINDEN

The Child's World

Published by The Child's World®
1980 Lookout Drive • Mankato, MN 56003-1705
800-599-READ • www.childsworld.com

Acknowledgments
The Child's World®: Mary Berendes, Publishing Director
The Design Lab: Design
Jody Jensen Shaffer: Editing
Pamela J. Mitsakos: Photo Research

Photos
Andres Rodriguez/Dreamstime.com: 22; Comstock/
Thinkstock.com: 6-7; deemac/iStock.com: 18;
dehooks/iStock.com: 15; E. Russell Primm: 9;
FourOaks/iStock.com: 20-21; Graffizone/iStock.
com: 10; jarenwicklund/iStock.com: 4; lakesides/
iStock.com: extinguisher; lisafx/iStock.com: 8;
monkeybusinessimages/iStock.com: 5; PhotoDisc:
design elements; Rubberball: 17; seanfboggs/iStock.
com: cover, 1; TFoxFoto/Shutterstock.com: 12, 14;
tiborgartner/iStock.com: 11

ISBN 9781626870130
LCCN 2013947291

Printed in the United States of America
Mankato, MN
December, 2013
PA02191

ABOUT THE AUTHOR

Dr. Cecilia Minden is a university professor and reading specialist with classroom and administrative experience in grades K–12. She earned her PhD in reading education from the University of Virginia.

CONTENTS

Hello, My Name Is Elizabeth.

Hello. My name is Elizabeth. Many people live and work in my neighborhood. Each of them helps the neighborhood in different ways.

I thought of all the things I like to do. I like to play team sports with my friends. I like being a leader. I always lend a hand when people need help. How could I help my neighborhood when I grow up?

I Could Be a Firefighter!

Firefighters bravely work together to help in emergencies. They are loyal to other members of their **firehouse** and to the neighborhood they serve. Best of all, firefighters save lives and property and help people stay safe!

When Did This Job Start?
Benjamin Franklin started the first fire-fighting company in 1736 in Philadelphia, Pennsylvania. New York City created its own company in 1737. More fire companies formed as the nation grew.

Learn About This Neighborhood Helper!

The best way to learn is to ask questions. Words such as *who*, *what*, *where*, *when*, and *why* will help me learn about being a firefighter.

Where Can I Learn More?
International Association of Firefighters
1750 New York Avenue NW
Washington, DC 20006

National Fire Academy
16825 South Seton Avenue
Emmitsburg, MD 21727

Asking a firefighter questions will help you learn more about the job.

Who Can Become a Firefighter?

Boys and girls who are good team players may want to become firefighters. People who want to be firefighters need to know how to work together. They also need to know how to take charge and be a leader during an emergency.

How Can I Explore This Job?

Many firehouses give tours to schoolchildren. Ask your teacher if he can arrange one. Ask the firefighters how they trained and what they like best about their work.

Firefighters are important neighborhood helpers. They keep homes and businesses safe. Firefighters also visit schools and community centers to teach their neighbors about preventing fires.

Firefighters often work with police officers to keep neighborhoods safe.

Meet a Firefighter!

This is Jon Kataoka. He is a firefighter in Chicago, Illinois. Jon loves being a firefighter. He says it is the best job in the world. Jon doesn't have any brothers or sisters, so he thinks of the people in his firehouse as his family.

How Many Firefighters Are There?
About 282,000 people work as firefighters.

Jon enjoys being a firefighter and is close to the people he works with.

Where Can I Learn to Be a Firefighter?

Men and women who are 21 years old and have graduated from high school can apply to become firefighters. Local fire departments offer a test for anyone qualified who wishes to become a firefighter.

Trained instructors teach new firefighters many things.

Firefighters use models during medical training. They practice how they will one day help real people during emergencies.

People who pass the test can take classes at a fire **academy**. Firefighters train there for three to six months, depending on the rules of their city or town. Jon studied at a fire academy and learned different ways to fight fires and rescue people. He also received medical training so he could help people in all kinds of emergencies.

How Much School Will I Need?

Firefighters learn their work at fire academies run by cities and towns. They learn in classrooms. They also are given physical training. Firefighters are always training to learn new techniques that may help them save lives.

Different types of hoses are used to fight different types of fires.

What Does a Firefighter Need to Do the Job?

Jon learned how to use special equipment when he trained at the fire academy. Some firefighters work with engine companies. A fire engine carries hoses. These hoses are different sizes. The large hoses are hooked up to fire hydrants, which supply water. Firefighters use smaller hoses to spray water on a fire.

Firefighters who work with truck companies are in charge of searching for people trapped in a fire and rescuing them. They are also

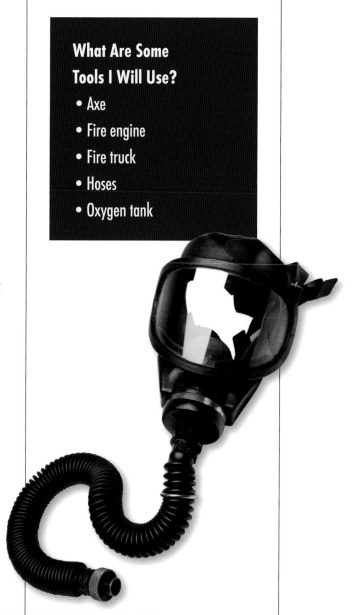

What Are Some Tools I Will Use?
- Axe
- Fire engine
- Fire truck
- Hoses
- Oxygen tank

Firefighters use masks to breathe fresh air during fires.

responsible for the **ventilation** of a fire. Firefighters have to get the bad air out and bring the good air in. They often go to the top of a burning building and saw a hole in the roof so the hot air and smoke can escape. Firefighters are trained to work with both engine and truck companies.

Firefighters use saws to cut open buildings for ventilation.

Where Does a Firefighter Work?

Jon looks at his fire station as "a home away from home." Many firefighters agree. This is why they call their fire station the firehouse. The firehouse is very similar to a regular home. There is a bunk room for sleeping, a TV room for relaxing, and a kitchen. All the firefighters take turns cooking for each other. There are some very good cooks at Jon's firehouse!

Jon gets to work at about 6:30 a.m. First, he checks out his gear to make sure everything will be ready

Firefighters learn to cook for large groups. Chili is a favorite!

to go if there's a fire. Next, there is roll call. This is when attendance is taken and Jon's captain tells everyone what is planned for the day. Each firefighter has certain chores. They are all responsible for keeping the firehouse clean and neat. Firefighters will also spend the day practicing different skills so they are ready for the next emergency.

The fire bell could ring at any moment. Jon and the other firefighters then stop what they are doing and go to the rescue!

Who Works with Firefighters?

Jon shares his firehouse with eleven other people. The captain is in charge of the firehouse. Another officer is the lieutenant. Five firefighters work on the engine, and another five work on the truck. Two travel with an ambulance. It is important for all the firefighters to support and protect each other.

Firefighters also often work with police and medical teams when there is an emergency. Everyone comes together during a rescue!

What other Jobs Might I Like?
- Emergency medical technician
- Fire inspector
- Lifeguard
- Park ranger

Medical workers work closely with firefighters to help people.

Firefighters often help protect family pets, too.

When Are Firefighters Pet Rescuers?

Firefighters are often asked to rescue a family's pets. One of Jon's firefighter friends went into a burning building to rescue a large dog. The animal went over to Jon's friend after the fire and rubbed against him as if to say thank you.

How Might My Job Change?
Firefighters gain experience and often move into more responsible positions. They usually have to take tests to get these better jobs. Some firefighters become fire inspectors. Fire inspectors try to find out the causes of fires.

I Want to Be a Firefighter!

I think being a firefighter would be a great way to be a neighborhood helper. Someday I may be the person who rescues you from a burning building!

Is This Job Growing?
The need for firefighters will grow as fast as other jobs.

Firefighters rescue people in all kinds of emergencies.

Why Don't You Try Being a Firefighter?

Do you think you would like to be a firefighter? It is very important for your family to have a plan of escape if there is a fire in your home. Ask your family to sit down with you and talk about the best way to escape from your home.

Pick a safe place outside for everyone to meet if there is a fire. You should practice your escape plans every month during a family fire drill.

Families need to work together during a fire, just like firefighters do.

GLOSSARY

academy (uh-KAD-uh-mee) a type of school

firehouse (FYER-hows) a fire station where firefighters work and keep their supplies

ventilation (ven-tuhl-AY-shun) the process of providing fresh air

LEARN MORE ABOUT FIREFIGHTERS

BOOKS

Demarest, Chris. *Firefighters A to Z.* New York: Aladdin Paperbacks, 2003.

Kalman, Bobbie. *Firefighters to the Rescue!* New York: Crabtree Publishing Co., 2004.

Kottke, Jan. *A Day with Firefighters.* Danbury, CT: Children's Press, 2000.

WEB SITES

Visit our home page for lots of links about firefighters:

www.childsworld.com/links

Note to Parents, Teachers, and Librarians: We routinely check our Web links to make sure they're safe, active sites—so encourage your readers to check them out!

INDEX